WHY PURSUE A DREAM?

ANNIE SHEORAN & ANAHITA SAIDI

Wonder House

(An imprint of Prakash Books)
Published by Wonder House Books
Wonder House Books is an imprint of Prakash Books
contact@wonderhousebooks.com
ISBN : 978-93-54404-85-6

Printed in India

Printed 2022

FOREWORD

My dear children, you own the most powerful and intricate instrument that no engineer or craftsman can ever replicate. This instrument is made up of your unique mind, your beautiful heart and your able body. Nothing is more precious than this instrument, which helps you dream and enables you to achieve what you dream of.

Dear children, I ask you to dream. Everything begins with a dream. Dream of the impossible. Dream of fulfilling your highest potential. Dream of creating a better world, and a better you.

Have a dream that complements your unique character. A noble dream encompasses joy, truth, altruism and peace. Formulate a dream, with genuine value and meaning, that is not simply a selfish wish but contributes to the goodness in society. Once you have a dream in your heart, I challenge you to pursue it with complete conviction and courage. It is only when intentions and hopes are put to determined and courageous action that impossible dreams come true. Having a dream is the mark of a person who will continue to grow throughout life.

If you ask me why you should pursue your dream, I will tell you that your dream gives you the power to be who you want to be, and to be the change you want to see. Those who give up on their dreams cause injury to their hearts and cannot enjoy profound fulfilment in their lives. Embrace and pursue your dreams, and continue advancing your noble and unique mission on this Earth.

Kailash Satyarthi
Nobel Peace Laureate

My grandpa asked me something new today,
"What do you want to be when you grow up?"
I told him I want to be an artist and an explorer! A ballerina! A scientist! An astronaut!
I want to be a teacher like mommy and a pilot like dad! I want to play basketball…

And he smiled, saying "You have a lot of dreams—pursue them courageously and remember you are strong.
You are smart.
You are brave.
And you can do anything you want."

I began to wonder about my dreams and what they really mean.
Why should I pursue my dreams?
I set out to explore these questions in my curious mind.

My mind is a beautiful place.
It is home to my imaginations and wildest thoughts.
My imaginations take me to faraway places,
and through these explorations, I start building my dreams.

My dreams are magical.
They make me happy.
I spend my days nurturing my dreams,
playing with them until they fill up my world with light and possibilities.

My dreams are a part of who I am.
They are my companions,
swirling around me all day long.
As I spend time with them, they become bigger and brighter.

But one day, my dreams flew away,
out of my window and onto the top of a tall mountain
far away in the distance.

Every night before I sleep, I look out the window and see the mountains.
As the sky gets darker, the mountains get brighter.
And if you look closely
at the tip of the tallest mountain,
I can almost see them—
the dreams I'm dreaming.

My dreams light up the sky with magic.
Through the darkness, they call out my name,
telling me to follow the light and find them.
But I can barely see the path,
and I'm scared to leave.

Inside is safe, and outside is stormy.
I hear a voice in my head saying,
Don't leave. It's too dark out.
You won't make it.

Should I stay home?

It's not scary in here,

but the voice of my heart is louder.

It tells me not to fear—

to follow the light and pursue my dreams.

Because these are my dreams! I built them and worked hard for them every day.

And most importantly, they make me truly happy.

So I take my first step
Full of courage in the pursuit of my dreams.

I am small, and the mountain is tall.
The strong winds are trying to push me down,
but they fail,
and I keep going forward,
jumping over every big rock and every pebble.

On the path to my dreams,
there are some steps and a few turns that make me feel lost
like I don't have any direction.
But then I remember, I don't need to be scared.
Because even after a few wrong steps and turns,
I am still closer to my dreams than I was from home.

There are different trails that lie ahead.
The road to my dreams is long and windy.
The other roads are shorter. Should I take the easier path?
But these other roads don't lead to my dreams,
And my momma once told me, "Sometimes the right path is not the easiest."
So I keep marching forward, full of courage in the pursuit of my dreams.

I can hear voices behind me,
telling me to stop and turn back,
that I won't make it up the path.
But I don't listen to them,
because what do they really know
about me and my pursuit of my dreams?
I may be small, but my courage is taller than the mountains.

It may be easier to give up.

It may be easier to go home.

But I can't stop thinking about my dreams.

They won't leave me.

They are mine.

They are me.

They make me proud.

They make me happy.

Sometimes I get scared and tired and lonely.

But then I remember

I am strong.

I am smart.
I am brave.

And I will reach my dreams.

But some steps are easier than others.
Some steps are not what they seem.
Some steps can knock me down.
Roses also come with thorns,
and friendly faces can still bite.

I stumble and fall many times,
but I stand up every time.
Because my dreams are my magic,
giving me direction and purpose—
helping me jump back up when I fall.

Our lives are what we make them to be.
Dreams become reality
when we pursue them courageously.
So I keep marching up the mountain

and closer to my dreams.

I finally make it to the mountain top!
Even after the long journey,
I am not tired.
I am not scared.
I feel different.
I feel a new energy inside me.

I was scared of the mountain, but I had no reason to fear.
It is not the mountain
but only the pebbles
that stood in my way.
And pebble by pebble, I can climb any mountain.

When I used to look at my dreams from my window,
I was scared of the storm.
But now I know,
after the rain comes the rainbow.
And no storm can stop me from pursuing my happiness, my dreams.

I run and grab my dreams.
I HUG THEM TIGHTLY and promise to never let go.
As I say these magical, and once what I thought impossible, words
I am struck by a flash of light from beyond the clouds.

I'm swirled into the sky,
and I feel a warm light beam from my skin.
The light from my dreams wraps around me, hugging me back.
I transform into my most magical, powerful, fierce, and fearless self
who can achieve any dream she wants.

I can change the world.

And all I have to do is remember to be myself.

After my journey, I realize that the light was in me all along

I just needed the courage to see it.

Now you ask me,

why pursue a dream?

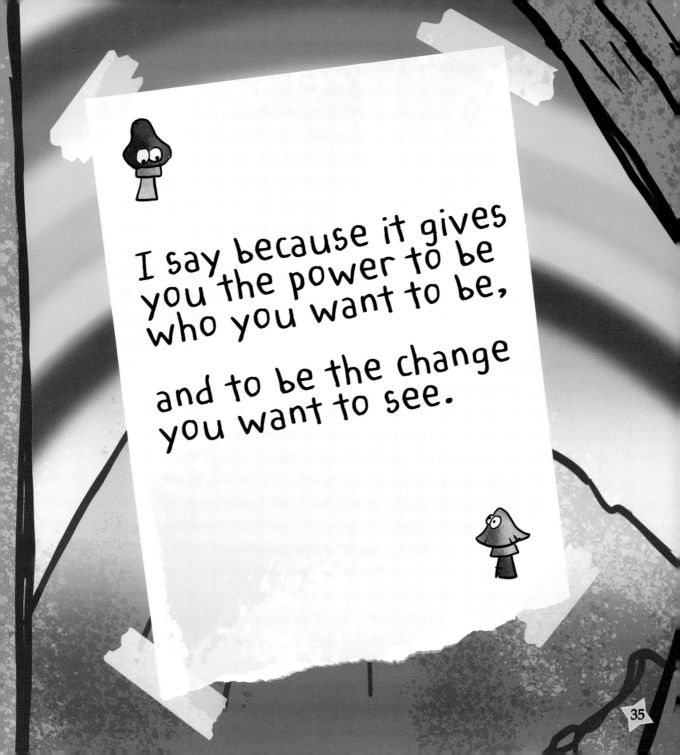

I say because it gives
you the power to be
who you want to be,

and to be the change
you want to see.

Our story follows a young girl as she sets out on a journey to follow her dreams, capturing the possibilities in a child's mind. She encounters obstacles in her path, but remains courageous throughout. The narrative inspires children to believe in themselves and pursue life boldly. The book breaks down life into a digestible philosophy—one that reframes the dreadful trek into a beautiful journey. Life is what you make it to be, and dreams become reality when you pursue them courageously.

Our foreword is written by Nobel Peace laureate Mr. Kailash Satyarthi, acclaimed for fighting for children's rights. It is penned as a letter encouraging children to pursue their dreams, for there is nothing more creative and powerful than a world visualized by children who dream without inhibition. The impossible becomes possible when a child dreams. Possibility becomes reality when a child's dream takes flight. The book is a reminder that every child matters and every dream matters. We want to use proceeds from the book to not only give back to Mr. Satyarthi's organization—Kailash Satyarthi Children's Foundation (satyarthi.org.in)—but also to create further projects of our own, incorporating the story and its lessons into programs that empower children to dream.